REAL ROMANS
digital time traveller

Mike Corbishley & Michael Cooper

Illustrated by Dai Owen

ENGLISH HERITAGE

TAG Learning Ltd
25 Pelham Road, Gravesend, Kent DA11 OHU

First published by TAG Learning Ltd 1999
in association with English Heritage
10 9 8 7 6 5 4 3 2 1

A CIP catalogue record for this book
is available from the British Library

ISBN 1 902 804 10 4

Reprographics by Scanhouse UK Ltd
Printed in Hong Kong/China by Wing King Tong

Acorn™, Change FSI™, Draw™, RISC OS™ and Paint™
Acorn Computers Ltd; AOL® America OnLine Inc; Apple™,
Mac™, Macintosh™ and Mac OS™ Apple Computer Inc;
ClarisWorks™ Claris Corporation; CompuServe™ ©
CompuServe Inc; Demon® Demon Internet Ltd; Fresco®
© ANT Ltd 1996; HyperStudio® © Roger Wagner Publishing
Inc; Microsoft Explorer™, MS Office™ and Windows™
Microsoft® Corporation, Paint © Microsoft® Corporation
1981; Plasticine™ Bluebird Toys UK Ltd; Netscape
Navigator® Netscape Communications Corporation 1994

The Real Romans team:

Text	Mike Corbishley, English Heritage
CD design & programming	Michael Cooper, emcee multimedia
Narrator	Joss Ackland
Book design	Alan McPherson
Technical co-ordinator	Tom Baird, TAG Learning Ltd
Editorial & book production	Clare Oliver, TAG Learning Ltd
Creative director	Tony Wheeler, TAG Learning Ltd
Cartoon illustrations	Dai Owen
Mosaics & tabula board	Ch'en Ling
Other illustrations	Peter Connolly, Philip Corke, Judith Dobie, Peter Dunn, Frank Gardiner, Ivan Lapper, Alan Sorrel, Richard Sorrel and Graham Sumner
Photography	all English Heritage Photo Library except for Colchester Archaeological Trust 34tr; Mike Corbishley 15tm&bl, 20tl, bl&bm, 21tl,bl&br, 30tr, 31tl, 34m, 38ml, 39tl; Norfolk Air Photograhs Library of the Norfolk Museums Service/Derek Edwards 37br; Dominic Powlesland 38mr, 39tr,ml, mr&br; Society of Antiquaries 33br; Roger White14tl&tr, 15tr, 20tr, 21tr, 30br, 36m

QuickTime

Contents

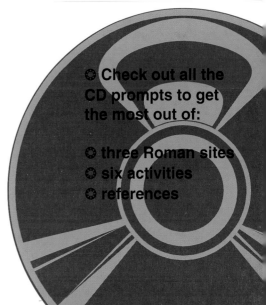

◉ Check out all the CD prompts to get the most out of:

◉ three Roman sites
◉ six activities
◉ references

About Real Romans

Real Romans is the first title in the *Digital Time Traveller* series of interactive, history resources. The book and CD have been designed to work together and provide everything you need to get started. On the CD-ROM you will find all sorts of exciting, useful things to help you to explore Roman Britain.

Top tours

Sit back and enjoy your own tour of each of the three Roman sites. The tours have been specially-recorded for the *Real Romans* CD-ROM so you can get as close in as you want.

Fantastic finds

Examine the evidence for yourself! Key objects discovered at the three Roman sites are on display in your own virtual museum.

Ace activities

There are six on-screen activities, including your own mosaic-making kit. Of course, there are loads more things to make and do in this book – for example, why not play a game of tabula with a friend? (See page XIX.) Time to get busy!

Crazy clip art

On the CD, you'll find lots of free clip art. How about making your own Roman-style greeting cards? With a little imagination, there's no limit to how you can use the pictures. (See page XLII.)

Wicked web sites

For those of you with access to the Internet, there is a selection of brilliant web sites to visit for more information about Roman times – all at the click of a button! (See page XLIV.)

System requirements

Check you have the right sort of computer to use the CD-ROM.

Getting started

Follow these instructions to load and run the *Real Romans* CD-ROM.

Windows users

If you have a Windows PC you will need:
- 486DX/90 MHz processor or better
- a VGA or SVGA monitor
- Windows '95 or higher
- CD-ROM drive
- sound card
- speakers or headphones
- 8MB available memory (RAM) (16MB recommended)

A printer, modem and Internet account will be useful for some of the on-screen activities.

You only need to install the CD once, but you will need to have the CD-ROM in your CD-drive each time you use *Real Romans*.
- Put the *Real Romans* CD into your CD-drive (with the label pointing up)
- Click on 'Start' in the task bar
- Click on 'Run' and type 'd:\setup' (where 'd' is the letter of your CD-drive)
- Click 'OK' or press 'enter'

Starting *Real Romans*
- Click on 'Start' in the task bar
- In Programs go to 'Romans CD'
- Double-click on 'Real Romans Start'

Apple Macintosh users

If you have an Apple Macintosh you will need:
- 040 processor or better
- System 7.1 or above
- 640 x 480 monitor set to 256 or more colours
- CD-ROM drive
- speakers (usually built-in) or headphones
- 8MB available memory (RAM)

A printer, modem and Internet account will be useful for some of the on-screen activities.

You do not need to install Real Romans. It runs directly from the CD-drive.
- Put the *Real Romans* CD into your CD-drive (with the label pointing up)
- Open the CD from the desktop
- Double-click on the 'Real Romans' icon

Acorn users

If you have an Acorn PC you will need:
- A7000 (minimum) or RISC PC
- RISC OS 3.1 or better
- 640 x 480 monitor with 256 or more colours
- CD-ROM drive
- speakers or headphones
- 8MB available memory (RAM)

A printer, modem and Internet account will be useful for some of the on-screen activities.

You do not need to install *Real Romans*. It runs directly from the CD-drive.
- Put the *Real Romans* CD into your CD-drive (with the label pointing up)
- Open the CD from the icon bar
- Double-click on '!Romans'

Using the CD-ROM

Finding your way around the CD-ROM is easy. Just click on the menu buttons and you will discover the main sections:

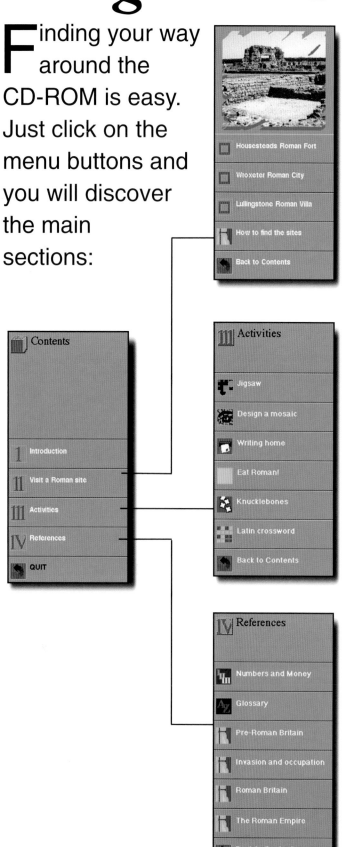

I Introduction

Click here for more information. You can get help by clicking on the contents button.

II Guided tours

Click here to visit the three Roman sites. You can choose to take a guided tour or explore each of the sites independently.

III Activities

Click here to select one of the on-screen activities. (Some have optional print-out facilities.)

IV References

Click here for additional information including maps and other references.

click here to listen to the guide

click here for more information

click here to see a site plan

click here to leave this site

click here to go back in time

click here to zoom in

which way you are pointing

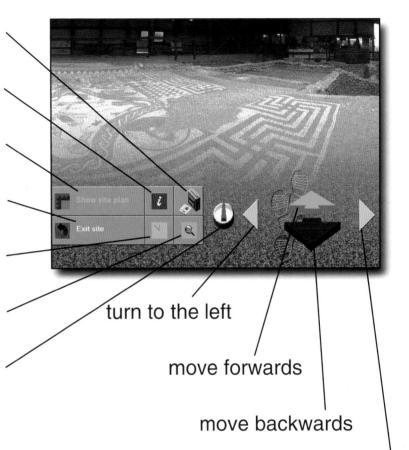

turn to the left

move forwards

move backwards

turn to the right

Moving around the Roman sites is easy. Just click on the arrow buttons to explore for yourself.

The CD also provides a library of useful clip art that you can use in your own work. This is in JPEG format and can be imported into other applications, such as MS Office or Paint on a Windows PC, ClarisWorks on a Macintosh, and !ChangeFSI, Draw or Paint on an Acorn. (See page XLII.)

There are also a number of useful Internet links, accessed directly from the *Real Romans* web page. (See page XLIV.) Always remember to tell an adult when you are going on-line.

Of course, the best way to find out about *Real Romans* is to sit back and explore…

VII

Who were the Romans?

From Britain to the Sahara Desert and from Portugal to Syria, the Romans eventually conquered lands in three continents.

In the 8th century BC, in the area where the city of Rome was later to be built, groups of farming people lived. The largest group was called the *Latini* – the Latins. This group of farmers became a world power and by the 2nd century AD the Romans had created a huge empire.

ABOUT 60 MILLION PEOPLE LIVED IN THE ROMAN EMPIRE!

animal skins

linen

purple dye

wool

silk

horses

wild animals

papyrus

glass

timber

ivory

pottery

marble

metals

fruit

wine

grain

olive oil

honey

fish sauce

spices

perfume

Roman trade

Every day, ships sailed into Ostia, the port of Rome, bringing a huge variety of goods from the provinces of the empire. Grain was delivered almost every day.

THE ROMANS BELIEVED THAT THEIR CITY WAS FOUNDED ON 21 APRIL 753BC.

BARBARIANS

THERE WAS A COURIER SERVICE, THE CURSUS PUBLICUS, TO CARRY OFFICIAL DOCUMENTS ALONG THE THOUSANDS OF ROADS ACROSS THE ROMAN EMPIRE.

BLACK SEA

FROM CHINA

ROME

MEDITERRANEAN SEA

FROM THE EAST

© Print out the map from the clip art showing all the provinces of the empire.

© Look at the maps of Roman Britain.

Verba et numeri*

All over the huge Roman empire, the official language was Latin.

But 60 million people lived in the Roman world and not all spoke or wrote Latin. The Roman empire was made up of lots of countries. Each had its own languages. If you wanted to get on in this Empire, then you needed to learn Latin and cope with their numbers. The Romans wrote in ink on a sort of paper called *papyrus* (made from flattened river plants), or on very thin slivers of wood.

They also made wax tablets and wrote on them with a sharp, metal instrument called a *stylus*.

Write a postcard home

Amaze your friends and relatives – try writing a postcard in Latin the next time you go on holiday! You will find a vocabulary list on your CD-ROM.

MAKE YOUR OWN ROMAN WRITING TABLET

MATERIALS

PLASTICINE

WAX

SKEWER

Ask an adult to melt the wax gently in an old saucepan

Make a shallow box like this from plasticine.

With care!

Melt wax in an old saucepan and pour carefully into the box.

Scratch your Latin words into the cooled, hard wax.

* Latin for 'words and numbers'

Roman numbers

The numbers we use today (1, 2, 3 and so on) came originally from India, but were adapted by the Arabs and used all over Europe. Roman numbers were quite different. The Romans used symbols to represent a few numbers.

Some clocks have Roman numbers.

modern	Roman	Latin
1	I	*uno*
2	II	*duo*
3	III	*tres*
4	IV	*quattuor*
5	V	*quinque*
6	VI	*sex*
7	VII	*septem*
8	VIII	*octo*
9	IX	*novem*
10	X	*decem*

I = 1   L = 50
V = 5   C = 100
X = 10   D = 500
M = 1,000

How to do it

If you want to write 17, you start with 10 (X) and add 5 (V) and then add 2 (II)

XVII

Simple!

If you want to write 46, you start with 50 (L) and put 10 (X) in front of it to take it away (XL) and then add 6 (VI)

XLVI

Simple!

Rules

Put a smaller number **in front** of a larger number and it subtracts it.

Put it **after** a larger number and it adds on to that number.

Kings and queens have Roman numbers after their name.

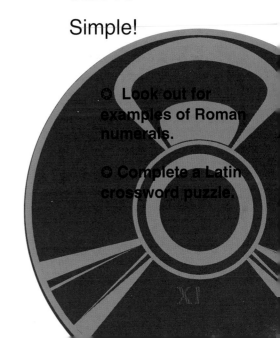

◎ Look out for examples of Roman numerals.

◎ Complete a Latin crossword puzzle.

The Romans arrive...

The Romans wanted to make Britain part of their empire but they had to cross the sea to invade.

The Roman general Julius Caesar made two attempts at invading Britain in 55 and 54BC. He brought his army from Gallia (now France) to investigate Britain. A hundred years later the Emperor Claudius led an invasion force which landed on the south coast. This time the army stayed on. Gradually the country was conquered and occupied. Roads, towns and farms were built.

55–54BC
Julius Caesar lands twice

AD43
Claudius invades with 40,000 men...

...and elephants!

Three Roman towns are destroyed

AD60
Queen Boudica leads a rebellion

This should keep out the barbarians!

AD78–83
Agricola, the Governor of Britain, invades Wales and the south of Scotland

Emperor Hadrian builds his famous wall

AD122

MAKE YOUR OWN TIMELINE

MATERIALS

PAPER

RULER

PENCIL OR PEN

SOME RELATIVES

Ask your relatives questions, eg. when were they born?

Collect picture ideas for your timeline. Use drawings or photos.

Pin up your results. Then why not try a holiday timeline?

...and stay a very long time

AD286–9
Carausius clears the English Channel of barbarians

AD305–6
Emperor Constantius fights a campaign in the north...

...and dies in York

I'll mint a coin in my honour

His son, the Emperor Constantine wins a victory

AD312–14

Picts!

Scots!

and Saxons!

Barbarian raids

AD364
Another barbarian attack is driven back

AD181–4
Tribes invade across the wall but are beaten back

AD367–8

Bye!

Troops are withdrawn to defend Italy

AD401–2

You must defend yourselves

AD410
Britain appeals to the Emperor Honorius for help

AD408

Saxon attack

The end of Britannia

The empire became so big that it became difficult for the Romans to defend its borders. Gradually they withdrew troops from the outer provinces such as Britain. The Romans were no longer in control.

○ Find the maps showing the Romans occupying more and more of Britain.

○ Investigate the northernmost frontier of the empire.

Life in the army

Whenever there was a new province to conquer, or a rebellion to put down, the Roman army swiftly came into action.

Roman soldiers were called legionaries because they were organised in large units called legions. A legion had 5,000 to 6,000 men in it.

THERE WERE ABOUT 450,000 ROMAN SOLDIERS IN THE EMPIRE.

The Emperor Trajan built this column in AD113 in Rome to record his victories.

Trajan's column: soldiers form a 'tortoise' to protect themselves from flying missiles.

Hadrian's Wall, northern Britain.

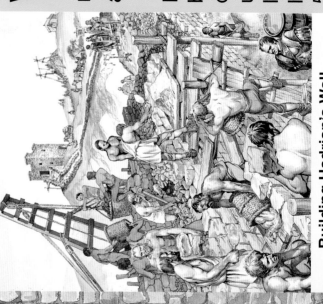

Building Hadrian's Wall.

The modern Ermine Street Guard form the 'tortoise'.

Reconstructed cavalry fort at the Lunt, Britain.

Arch in Rome, built by the Emperor Constantine to celebrate his victories in war.

A soldier carried 30 kilograms of gear – and rations – enough for three days on the march. The army included engineers to straighten out roads and build bridges. Each time they stopped, the soldiers built temporary camps and slept in tents. When a legion was on permanent duty, for example at Hadrian's Wall, forts were built. A legionary soldier had to do more than just fight the enemy. He went on regular patrols and guarded important places such as quarries, or river and frontier crossings.

Reconstructed main gate of the fort at Saalburg, Germany.

Wallsend Roman fort, Hadrian's Wall.

FOCUS ON...Housesteads a Roman fort

Housesteads Fort was part of the defended northern frontier of Roman Britain.

The Emperor Hadrian made an official tour of Britain in AD122. We think he ordered the great wall, now known as Hadrian's Wall, to be built across the north of the

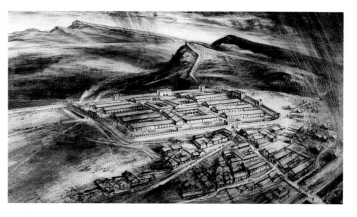

This is an artist's impression of what Housesteads may have looked like in the 3rd century AD.

HADRIAN'S WALL RAN FOR 80 ROMAN MILES (117 KM) FROM WALLSEND ON THE RIVER TYNE TO BOWNESS ON THE SOLWAY FIRTH.

province, from sea to sea. Along it were a number of forts, and look-out posts. The aim of all this defence was to stop peoples further north from invading or raiding Roman territory.

MAKE YOUR OWN ROMAN SHIELD

MATERIALS

CARD

SCISSORS

GLUESTICK

PAINTS
AND BRUSHES

Safe as houses!

Cut a rectangle and two thin, long strips from card.

Glue the strips to pull the shield into a curved shape.

Decorate with a Roman design – or make up your own.

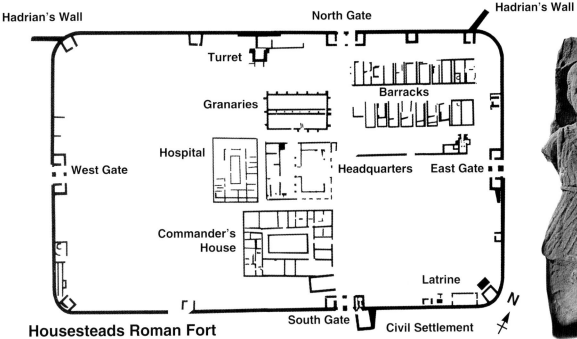

Hadrian's Wall North Gate Hadrian's Wall
Turret
Granaries
Barracks
Hospital
Headquarters East Gate
West Gate
Commander's House
Latrine
South Gate Civil Settlement
N

Housesteads Roman Fort

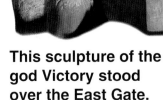

This sculpture of the god Victory stood over the East Gate.

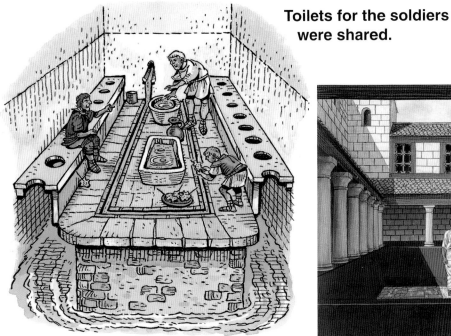

Toilets for the soldiers were shared.

Inside the fort, the commander of the troops lived in a grand house.

The soldiers stationed on Hadrian's Wall did not spend much time fighting, but lots of time training or on cleaning duty! Patrolling the territory was important, either along the Wall or in the lands to the north. Time off could be spent in the shops and taverns just outside the fort.

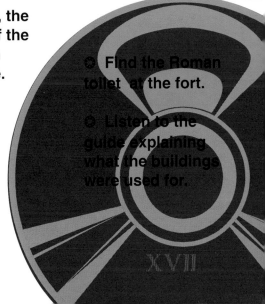

◎ Find the Roman toilet at the fort.

◎ Listen to the guide explaining what the buildings were used for.

XVII

Pueri, puellae et ludi*

To a Roman, the Latin word *ludi* meant different sorts of games – from a board game to a gladiator fight in the amphitheatre.

Gladiators were so called because some carried a *gladius*, a short sword. Others were armed only with a net and spear.

Toys

Children had some of the same games and toys as children today. They had marbles and miniature people and animals made of clay. Outside, there were games with hoops and balls.

Playing ball

The game of *trigon* was for three players who threw hard, leather balls to each other. *Harpastum* was another ball game, rather like rugby.

This carved, stone board game was discovered on Hadrian's Wall. It has counters, dice and shaker pots.

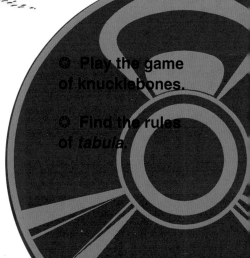

- Play the game of knucklebones.
- Find the rules of *tabula*.

*Latin for 'boys, girls and games'.

Mosaic from Pompeii, Italy.

From a statue of the Emperor Constantine, Rome.

Life in a Roman town

Many Romans travelled long distances across their own provinces, or even across the whole Roman Empire.

Romans expected to travel on reasonably straight roads between one town and the next. As they approached a town, they first passed through cemeteries with the impressive tombs of the town's rich citizens.

LEAD PIPES BROUGHT WATER TO FOUNTAINS IN THE STREET.

Pantheon, Rome. Temple to all the Roman gods.

Aqueduct at Pont du Gard, France.

Lodging house, Wall, Britain.

Roman temple, Nîmes, France.

Gladiators at Silchester, Britain.

Colosseum amphitheatre, Rome.

Some towns were fortified with strong, stone walls and gates, that were closed and guarded at night. Inside the walls, the town was laid out in a very regular way. The streets were straight, crossing each other at right angles. As well as houses and shops, there were impressive public buildings – the forum, where town business took place and markets were held, temples, public baths and, perhaps, a theatre.

SOME TOWNS HAD AN AMPHITHEATRE. HERE, GLADIATORS FOUGHT ANIMALS, OR EACH OTHER!

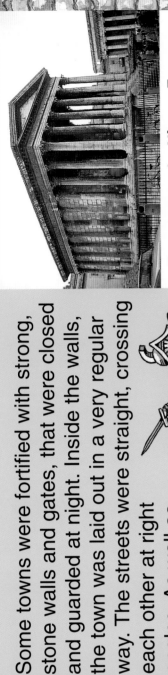

Roman tombstone.

Street in Pompeii, Italy.

FOCUS ON... Wroxeter a Roman city

Wroxeter, near Shrewsbury in the West Midlands, was once an important Roman city.

Wroxeter began life as a Roman fort, like Housesteads. When the army pulled out, the Romans decided to make this place the town for the local people, called the *Cornovii.*

This is what Wroxeter may have looked like in the 2nd century. It was the fourth-largest town in Roman Britain.

FOUR LOCALS WERE TAKEN TO COURT FOR DIGGING UP ROMAN TREASURE IN 1292.

MAKE YOUR OWN ROMAN SANDALS

MATERIALS

CARD

A FRIEND

PENCIL

SCISSORS

SHOELACES

Ask a friend to draw round each of your feet on the card.

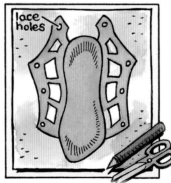

Draw the tops of the sandals around each foot outline.

Cut out carefully, thread with laces – and wear!

XXII

The forum at Wroxeter was where the town's business was conducted.

The Emperor Hadrian may have visited Wroxeter on his tour of the province in AD122. The main public buildings – the forum and the baths – were finished shortly afterwards.

Only Roman citizens (and only men) were allowed to wear the *toga*. It was a semi-circular piece of cloth over 5.5m long.

modern road

North Aisle

Basilica

South Aisle

Forum

Snack bar

Snack bar

Latrine

Entrance

Market

Pool

Caldarium

Laconica

Frigidarium

Tepidarium

Laconica

Caldarium

Furnace

N

The public baths

Investigate the baths for yourself.

Use this page as you tour the baths.

Having a bath

The public baths in a Roman town were not just for getting clean in! They were important places for relaxing, seeing friends or even holding business meetings.

Some baths had separate facilities for men and women. If not, there were special times set aside for each sex. A large number of slaves were needed to keep the baths going. There were all sorts of jobs for them to do – keeping the baths clean and the fires stoked, serving snacks and drinks, bringing towels, giving a massage or even plucking hair from the armpits of customers! An essential job was to scrape the customers clean after a hot, steamy bath or exercise.

tweezers

oil and strigil

ear scoop

clogs for hot floors

Next you are ready for the *Caldarium* (hot room)

a hip bath

steam cleaned the skin

Then a massage

While below...

scraping the skin clean with a strigil

The furnace provided the heat for the baths

Pecunia et nummi*

The Romans introduced their system of money into all the provinces they governed.

They minted coins, just as countries do today, but they didn't have paper money. Their coins carried the head of the emperor on the front, with some sort of message or important event recorded on the back. Each emperor wanted to show that he had come to power. Coins were a way of showing people all over the empire what he looked like!

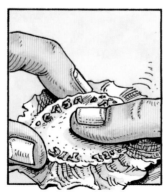

CELTIC PEOPLE IN BRITAIN HAD BEEN MINTING THEIR OWN COINS FOR AT LEAST 300 YEARS BEFORE THE ROMANS ARRIVED!

Modern coins

Some countries today use the same sorts of inscriptions on their coins as the Romans did.

Britain: Britannia, 1944

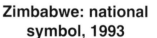

Britain: Queen Victoria, 1900

USA: American eagle, 1988

Zimbabwe: national symbol, 1993

Greece: ancient Greek ship, 1990

MAKE YOUR OWN ROMAN COIN

MATERIALS

REPLICA ROMAN COIN

TINFOIL

SCISSORS

CARD

GLUESTICK

Place the foil over one side of the coin. Rub firmly.

Make a rubbing of the other side. Cut out both rubbings.

Cut a coin-sized card circle. Glue on the rubbings.

*Latin for 'coins and money'

Cracking the code

Roman coins have letters which have been shortened from the original word in Latin. They also have numbers and letters which are a sort of code and, if translated, can tell you when the coin was minted. You can find a lot of detail by looking at the coin carefully...

TICLAVD. CAESAR. AVG. PM. TRPIIII

AVG
is short for Augustus, another name for emperor after the first emperor of Rome, Augustus

CAESAR
is a word for emperor taken from Julius Caesar
(see page XII)

PM
is short for Pontifex Maximus which means Claudius was Rome's Chief Priest

TI CLAVD
gives the emperor's name – Tiberius Claudius

TR·P·IIII
is short for Tribunicia IIII which means that Claudius held the post of Chief Minister for the fourth time

So, when was the coin minted? Because there was a careful record kept of all posts held by government officials and emperors, we know that this coin was minted in AD44–45, just after the Emperor Claudius invaded Britain.

● Find out what coins were worth and how much dormice cost.

● What were the Latin names of the four Roman coins?

Dormouse and chips?

Yes, the Romans did eat dormice! But they certainly didn't have chips.

Why? Because potatoes were not brought into Europe from America until the 1500s. The Romans ate meat, fish and vegetables as we do today and they liked strong flavourings in their food. The Romans usually had three meals a day. As soon as it got light, the family got up and ate breakfast. This was a meal of bread and fruit called the *ientaculum*. Lunch was a light meal at midday of cold meat, fish, vegetables and bread. They called this meal the *prandium*. The main meal of the day, called the *cena*, began around 4 o'clock. Its courses could go on into the evening.

SOME ROMAN FEASTS INCLUDED ROAST SWANS!

THE MOST POPULAR SAUCE WAS LIQUAMEN. IT WAS MADE FROM THE INSIDES OF FISH, WHICH WERE DRIED IN THE SUN, THEN POUNDED UP!

MAKE YOUR OWN ROMAN SWEETS

MATERIALS

WHOLE DATES

KNIFE

CHOPPED NUTS

SALT

RUNNY HONEY

Cut on a flat surface

Make a small cut and take the stone out of each date.

Fill each date with nuts or pine kernels. Then roll in salt.

I hope my friends don't mind sticky fingers!

Pour over some delicious runny honey – and dig in!

Looking through to the dining room at Lullingstone

DORMICE FOR EATING WERE KEPT IN A POT AND FATTENED UP ON NUTS. DON'T TRY IT TODAY – DORMICE ARE A PROTECTED SPECIES!

The Latin word for a dining room is *triclinium*. The word means three seats. This is because the main meal of the day was served on low tables in front of three low benches. Diners reclined on these to eat.

A Roman recipe book

A real Roman recipe book written by Apicius still exists. To show how many different sorts of flavouring the Romans liked, here is the recipe for boiled cabbage:

ARRANGE THE BOILED CABBAGES IN A SHALLOW PAN AND DRESS THEM WITH FISH SAUCE, OIL, WINE AND CUMIN. THEN SPRINKLE WITH PEPPER, CHOPPED LEEKS, CARAWAY SEEDS AND FRESH CORIANDER.

✪ Investigate the dining room at Lullingstone Roman Villa.

✪ Print out some real Roman recipes and try them out.

Life in the country

Today the word 'villa' often means a house by the seaside, perhaps in a foreign country.

To the Romans, *villa* could mean a farm or a holiday house by the sea, in the countryside or in the mountains. The Roman poet Martial said, *'Whenever I'm worn out with worry and want to get some rest, I go to my villa'.*

AMPHORAE WERE VERY LARGE STORAGE JARS!

Gargrave Roman Villa in the late 3rd century AD.

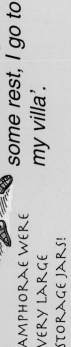

Emperor Hadrian's villa at Tivoli, near Rome.

A reconstructed Roman villa at Mehring, Germany.

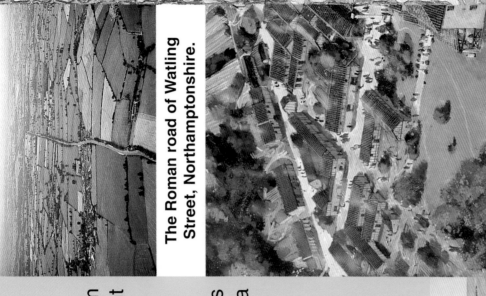

The Roman road of Watling Street, Northamptonshire.

Staging post on Watling Street at Wall, Staffordshire.

Farms, some of them huge, produced the food needed for the millions who lived in the towns. A rich Roman might own a number of villa estates in different provinces. He employed a farm manager, called a *vilicus*. His wife might be the *vilica* – the housekeeper in charge of the household slaves. Many Roman farms grew a variety of crops, such as wheat, vines, olives and fruit, and kept a range of animals for food.

THE ROMANS GREW CARROTS, LETTUCES, CABBAGES, PARSNIPS, PEAS, RADISHES AND TURNIPS.

Lullingstone Roman Villa, Kent.

Part of the landscape of Roman Britain around AD200.

FOCUS ON...Lullingstone
a country villa

The villa at Lullingstone in Kent was just one of hundreds built by rich farmers during the early years of the Roman occupation of Britain.

Before the Romans arrived, Celtic farmers lived at what was later to be called Lullingstone. The first Roman farm building was put up 40 years after the invasion.

Most of the families who lived here were farmers. But some people owned houses here so they could

This is an artist's impression of what Lullingstone may have looked like in the 4th century AD.

take a break from their official duties in the capital Londinium (London).

MAKE YOUR OWN ROMAN VILLA

MATERIALS

CARD

PENCIL

SCISSORS

GLUESTICK

Print the plan of Lullingstone villa from the CD-ROM.

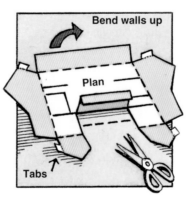

Copy the plan on card and add walls and roof. Cut out.

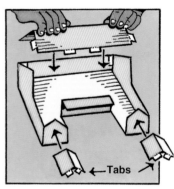

Glue the tabs to assemble your Roman villa.

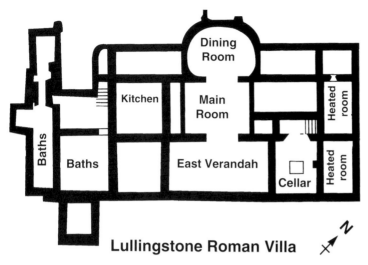

Lullingstone Roman Villa

This is the mosaic floor of the dining room at Lullingstone. Look back to page XXIX to see how the room might have looked.

Mosaic floors

Lullingstone is famous today for its mosaic floors. An enormous amount of time must have gone into making up the patterns and 'drawing' out the pictures.

You can see how it was done on page XXXV.

Discovering Lullingstone

Archaeologists began excavating the villa at Lullingstone in 1949. By 1963 the site was open to visitors.

This is one of the rooms during excavation, showing the marble busts of the ancestors of one of the villa's owners.

Fin... ...om ...re ...e busts ...iscovered.

...ch of the ...mob... ...und ...e s...

XXXIII

Artis opus*

The Romans enjoyed art and liked to see it in their houses and in their public buildings.

A fragment of wall painting found at Colchester, showing a gladiator.

Sculpture

Sculptors were in great demand throughout the empire. They made statues of gods, tombstones and busts of people's ancestors. They also created a lot of carved decoration for public buildings.

Wall paintings

The Romans decorated their rooms with patterns and pictures painted straight on to the plaster walls. Artists usually used the fresco technique – the paint was applied before the plaster had dried.

MAKE YOUR OWN ROMAN MOSAIC

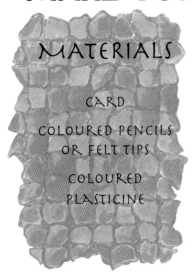

MATERIALS

CARD

COLOURED PENCILS OR FELT TIPS

COLOURED PLASTICINE

Sketch the design for your mosaic on to the card.

Shape 1-cm cubes from different-coloured plasticine.

Use the cubes as *tesserae* to fill in your design.

* Latin for 'work of art'

The large mosaic at Lullingstone showed the four seasons (see page XXXIII). This one is 'Summer'.

Mosaic at Aldborough Roman Town, North Yorkshire.

Roman mosaics

Perhaps the most famous of all types of Roman art is the mosaic. Mosaics, which could be on floors or walls, were made from lots of little cubes of stone or tile. These cubes were called *tesserae*. Using thousands of them, mosaic artists created pictures as detailed as paintings.

IT TOOK ABOUT 15 MILLION TESSERAE TO LAY A FLOOR 15M SQUARE.

❂ Design and print your own mosaic.

❂ How many works of art can you find at the three sites?

Discovering the past

P eople have been searching for centuries to discover the evidence for the past. Today archaeologists use all sorts of high-tech techniques to search out those clues.

WE STILL USE ROMAN ROUTES TODAY, BUT THE ROADS ARE FAR BELOW US!

Recycled Romans

One of the first places archaeologists look for evidence of the Romans is in later buildings! In the time after the Romans, many buildings were re-used for something else.

Ancient and modern

You will often be walking 5m above Roman streets in some towns in Britain. There are good examples in Colchester (the first capital of Roman Britain), London, York and Lincoln.

These flats in Lucca, Italy are built into a Roman amphitheatre.

MAKE YOUR OWN CROP-MARK

MATERIALS

SEED TRAY
STONES
POTTING COMPOST
SOIL
CRESS SEEDS

Build one wall of stones and another of potting compost.

Fill the tray with soil and plant the cress seeds evenly.

Your crop should do better over the compost.

Walking the fields

Archaeologists often walk over ploughed fields (with permission of course) to look for evidence of the past. Ploughing sometimes brings buried bits and pieces from the past to the surface.

The archaeological team carefully marks the field into numbered squares. They collect and label everything they find.

Aerial photography

The most important of the archaeologist's scientific techniques is aerial photography. Looking at the ground from an aeroplane gives archaeologists the opportunity to see where crops are growing above buried remains.

Crop-marks

Crops (such as wheat, barley, sugar beet, potatoes and grass) often grow better over buried features, such as ditches. On the other hand, crops growing over walls or floors might not do so well.

Archaeologists often use black and white film to capture the evidence of crop-marks more clearly.

This amazing photo shows a Roman villa. It has had wings added to it like Lullingstone.

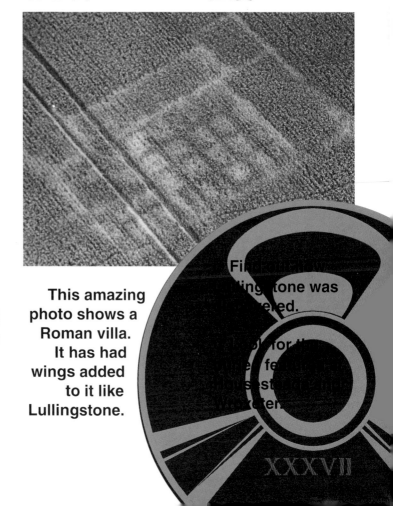

XXXVII

Excavation and recording

Archaeologists often have to excavate – or dig – sites that are threatened with destruction from new building or ploughing.

Experts in different skills make up an archaeological excavation team. Some dig the site, while others record the finds, by drawing, writing notes and taking photographs. Every last scrap of evidence has to be carefully uncovered

and recorded. The team examine everything, from the walls and floors to the rubbish pits and foundations. Computerised systems of recording are often used on the site itself. During the excavation, archaeologists will find a lot of objects, including broken pots, seeds, and even animal bones.

The basilica at Wroxeter during excavation.

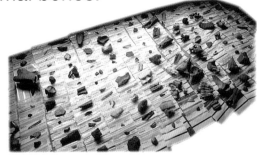

All objects are carefully cleaned and numbered.

MAKE YOUR OWN EXCAVATION

MATERIALS

SEED TRAY

POTTING COMPOST

SPOON

PAINT BRUSH

PLASTICINE

A FRIEND

In the tray, build the 'ruins' for your site out of plasticine.

Cover your archaeological site with compost.

Ask a friend to carefully excavate the site.

Excavation requires skill...and patience.

Archaeologists have to excavate skeletons! The numbers and letters identify where it was found on the site.

Archaeologists make detailed drawings of areas of the site.

This is the excavated skeleton of a hunting dog. The marked rule shows the size of the bones for future reference.

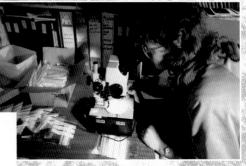

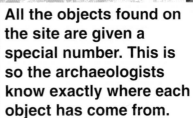

All the objects found on the site are given a special number. This is so the archaeologists know exactly where each object has come from.

Complete blocks of soil are lifted to be excavated later in a laboratory. Far more detail can be recovered here than in the open air.

◉ Find the photographs of the excavations at Lullingstone.

◉ Look out for the different types of objects found at the three sites.

XXXIX

Partes et fragmenta*

You can only really find out about the Romans by looking for evidence. The clues to how they lived are hidden in all sorts of things.

But there is a problem with looking for clues. Finding out about the past is like doing a jigsaw puzzle – but with some (or maybe many) of the pieces missing. Archaeologists and historians have to guess at those missing areas. You can be a history detective, too.

Writing

One way of discovering the Romans is by reading what they wrote (or at least, an English translation!) Here are two very different examples:

One Roman writer said that Julius Caesar (the great dictator and invader of Britain)

...WAS A BIT OF A DANDY. HE ALWAYS KEPT HIS HAIR CAREFULLY TRIMMED AND USED TO COMB HIS FEW HAIRS FORWARD TO COVER HIS BALDNESS.

One soldier stationed on Hadrian's Wall got this letter (only part survives) with a parcel from home,

I HAVE SENT YOU...PAIRS OF WOOLLEN SOCKS, TWO PAIRS OF SANDALS AND TWO PAIRS OF UNDERPANTS...

*Latin for 'bits and pieces.'

Looking at objects

Some objects from the past are a mystery to us simply because we don't use them today. Would you be able to work out what a *strigil* was if you hadn't already found out on page XXIV? But archaeologists usually find fragments of objects, rather than the whole object.

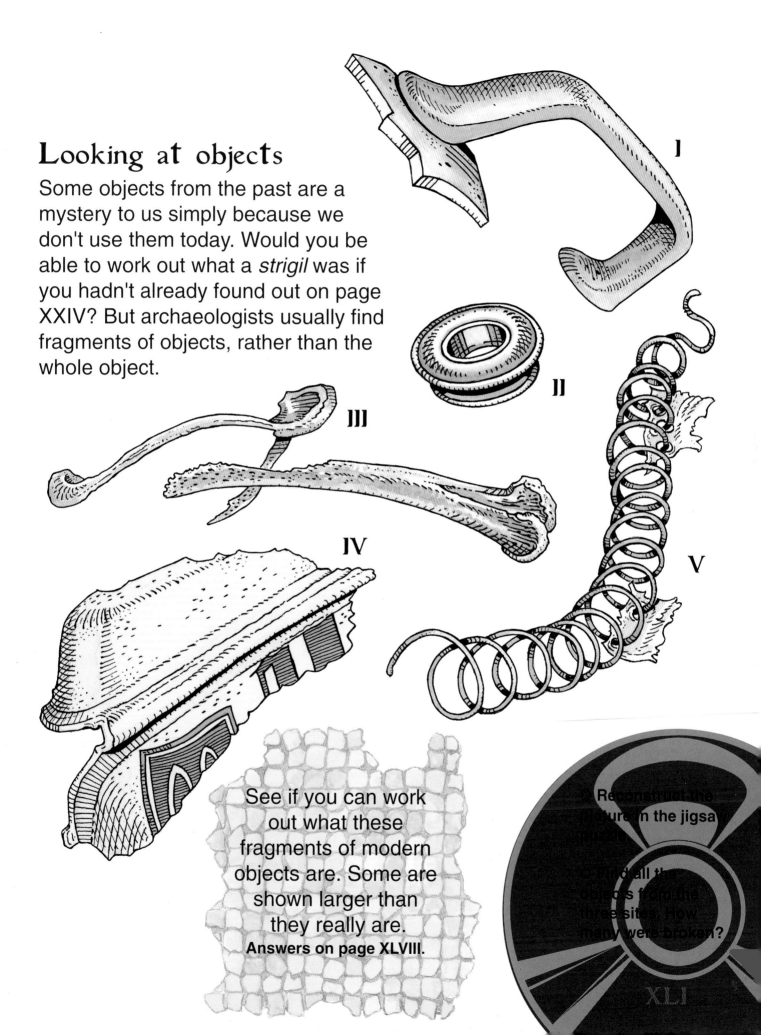

I

II

III

IV

V

See if you can work out what these fragments of modern objects are. Some are shown larger than they really are.
Answers on page XLVIII.

● Reconstruct the picture in the jigsaw puzzle.

● Find all the objects from the three sites. How many were broken?

XLI

Real Roman clip art

These images are all stored in a folder called 'Clip Art' on the *Real Romans* CD.

You can import or insert the clip art directly into your word processor from the 'File' menu. Alternatively, if you have an application that loads JPEG files directly, such as Internet Explorer, simply double-click on a clip art file. On an Acorn you can also drag and drop the files on to the work area of a suitable application, such as Draw.

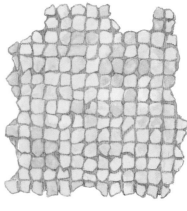

The Roman Empire

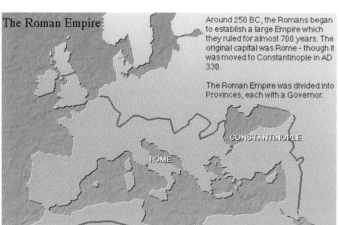

Around 250 BC, the Romans began to establish a large Empire which they ruled for almost 700 years. The original capital was Rome - though it was moved to Constantinople in AD 330.

The Roman Empire was divided into Provinces, each with a Governor.

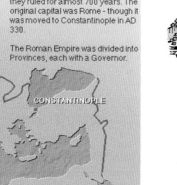

● **What other pieces of clip art can you find in the clip art folder?**

XLIII

Real Romans on the web

If you have an Internet connection you can find out lots more about the Romans on-line. This section contains a selection of useful links to important Roman web sites.

You will need

- a modem connected to your PC
- a Web Browser
  (such as Netscape Navigator, Microsoft Explorer or !Fresco)
- an Internet service connection
  (such as Demon or AOL)

- Launch your browser and connect up to the Internet
- Type in
  'http://www.tagdev.co.uk/realromans
- Choose from the list of links and find out lots more about the Romans

School sites

Roman Times
Nettlesworth Primary School
Pictures and information on a range of Roman topics

Country Life in Roman Britain
The Glynne School
Samples of work on a visit to Wroxeter

Report on Visit to Hadrian's Wall
Netherhall School
Description of a visit to Hadrian's wall

Sites for children

Hadrian's Wall and the Romans
Northumberland County Council
Pictures, information and links about visiting Hadrian's Wall

Exploring the Wall
Northumbria Tourist Board
Pictures, information, maps and links about Hadrian's Wall

About the Wall
Northumbria Tourist Board
Pictures, information, maps and links about Hadrian's Wall

Britannia
Ancient Sites Online
Pictures and information on a range of Roman topics

Roman Baths Virtual tour
Somerset Council
Pictures, maps and information on the Roman Baths Museum and Pump Room

Roman Museum
The Museum of the Potteries, Stoke on Trent
Lots of useful information and pictures on a range of Roman topics

Roman Pictures
Hope Education
Useful selection of Roman line drawings

The Forum Virtual tour
Think Quest
Interactive tour of the different buildings in the Roman Forum, plus lots of pictures and information

The Ermine Street Guard
University of Newcastle-upon-Tyne
Pictures and information about this group who research and reconstruct Roman armour and equipment

Young Archaeologists club
Council for British Archaeology
Information about the club

British Museum
British Museum home page
Information about the museum's galleries, exhibitions and events

Sites for teachers and parents

Hadrian's Wall and the Romans
Northumberland County Council
Pictures, information and links about visiting Hadrian's Wall

Hadrian's Wall
Northumbria Tourist Board
Pictures, information, maps and links about Hadrian's Wall

Roman Baths Teachers' Page
Somerset Council
Pictures, maps and information on the Roman Baths Museum and Pump Room

The Forum Romanum Title Page
Think Quest
Interactive tour of the different buildings in the Roman Forum, plus lots of pictures and information

Excavations at Isthmia
The Ohio State University
Information on the archaeological excavations at the site at Isthmia, plus pictures and links

Roman Military Sites of Britain
Peter Green
An introduction to military sites built by the Roman Army in Britain, with pictures, site plans and information

Wroxeter Hinterland Tours
Birmingham University
Reports on this three-year archaeological study of the Wroxeter site, with pictures, maps, diagrams and lots of information

Hadrian's Wall Museums
English Heritage
Information on the various museums relating to Hadrian's Wall, plus pictures

Athena Review
Athena Review
Journal of Archaeology, History, and Exploration
Pictures, links and information

English Heritage
English Heritage home page
Pictures, links and information for sites across the country

TAG Developments Ltd
TAG's home page
Information about other software, resources and training

Link sites

Greek and Roman Sightseeing
Bellum Catilinae
A privately-supported listing of sites relating to the Classics, plus links to Roman sites around the world

Britmus1 links
Athena Review
Journal of Archaeology, History, and Exploration
Romano-British Sites and Museums (part 1):
a guide to Roman forts and related museums

Britmus2 links
Athena Review
Journal of Archaeology, History, and Exploration
Romano-British Sites and Museums (part 2):
a guide to towns, villas, and regional museums

The Ancient World
Web links
If you can't find what you're looking for at any of these sites, you could make your own search:
1. Launch your browser and connect up to the Internet
2. Type in 'http://www.yahoo.com'
3. Type in some words to make your search
    roman villa
    roman army
    roman empire

WARNING
The Internet is a public place and you need to be careful when you are exploring. Never go on-line without the permission of a parent or teacher.

Glossary

AMPHITHEATRE 'theatre in the round' used for gladiatorial and animal fights

 AMPHORAE huge, pottery jars used to transport and store wine, olive oil or fish sauce

APODYTERIUM changing room in the baths

AQUEDUCT overground water channel often raised on arches over rivers or ravines

ARCHAEOLOGIST scientist who collects and interprets evidence from the past

BASILICA long building with aisles used for meetings, law courts or exercise

CALDARIUM the hot room of the public baths

 CENA main meal of the day

CROP-MARK mark, usually visible only from the air, showing the location of buried features

CURSUS PUBLICUS the official courier service for important documents

DICTATOR appointed in times of emergency to run the government and the army

EMPEROR from the Latin word *imperator* meaning 'commander-in-chief'; used from the time of the Emperor Augustus to mean 'supreme ruler of the empire'

EMPIRE large group of countries ruled by one person

EVIDENCE written or physical remains which gives clues to the story of the past

FORUM large open space in the centre of a town, used for markets and meetings; public buildings were usually grouped in and around it

FRIGIDARIUM the cold, unheated, room of the public baths

 GLADIATOR professional warrior who fought to the death in the amphitheatre

GLADIUS short, stabbing sword carried by Roman soldiers

IENTACULUM a light breakfast taken at dawn

LATIN the official language of the Roman empire

LEGION the main unit of the Roman army

LEGIONARIES the name for Roman soldiers, taken from the word *legion*

LIQUAMEN fish sauce used to flavour many Roman dishes

MOSAIC wall or floor decoration made up of *tesserae*

PAPYRUS 'paper' made from the flattened stems of the papyrus reed

PRANDIUM a light meal taken at midday

PROVINCE area or country taken over and governed by the Romans

STRIGIL curved instrument for scraping oil from the skin during bathing

STYLUS instrument, sharpened at one end, used to write letters and numbers on a wax writing tablet

TEPIDARIUM the warm room of the baths

TESSERAE small pieces of stone, tile or glass used to make mosaics

TOGA outer garment that could only be worn by a Roman citizen

TRICLINIUM dining room in a house

VILLA farming estate, or house in the country or by the sea

VILICUS farm manager

VILICA housekeeper of a country estate

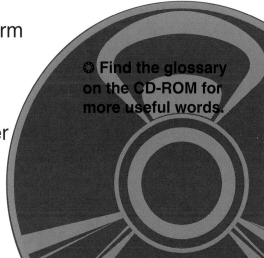

Find the glossary on the CD-ROM for more useful words.

Useful addresses

English Heritage
23 Savile Row
London W1X 1AB

TAG Developments Ltd
25 Pelham Road
Gravesend
Kent DA11 OHU

Young Archaeologists Club
Bowes Morrell House
111 Walmgate
York YO1 9WA

The three English Heritage sites are:

Housesteads Roman Fort
Northumberland, north-east of Bardon Mill

Lullingstone Roman Villa
Kent, south-west of Eynsford

Wroxeter Roman City
Shropshire, east of Shrewsbury

The fragments of objects on page XLI were

I   handle of a cup
II   eyelet from a pair of trainers
III broken chicken bones
IV   piece of a hamburger box
V   metal spiral from a notepad

Did you guess them all correctly?

Museums to visit

The Romans occupied most of Britain and left behind thousands and thousands of remains! Many of them have been discovered by archaeologists and are now on display in museums around the country. Try your local museum or ask at the library for information. Here are the addresses of a few museums with really good collections of Roman material which you might like to visit:

Cardiff: The National Museum of Wales, Cathays Park, Cardiff CF1 3NP

Chester: The Grosvenor Museum, 27 Grosvenor Street, Chester, Cheshire CH1 2DD

Cirencester: The Corinium Museum, Park Street, Cirencester, Gloucestershire GL7 2BX

Colchester: The Castle Museum, Castle Park, Colchester, Essex CO1 1TJ

Edinburgh: Royal Museum of Scotland and Museum of Scotland, Chambers Street, Edinburgh EH1 1JF

Fishbourne: Fishbourne Roman Palace, Salthill Road, Fishbourne, nr Chichester, West Sussex PO19 2QR

Leicester: The Jewry Wall Museum, St Nicholas Circle, Leicester LE1 4LB

Lincoln: Lincoln City and County Museum, 12 Friars Lane, Lincoln LN2 5AL

London: The British Museum, Great Russell Street, London WC1B 3DG

London: The Museum of London, London Wall, London EC2Y 5HN

Newcastle-upon-Tyne: The Museum of Antiquities, The University, Newcastle Upon Tyne, NE1 7RU

Reading: Reading Museum and Art Gallery, The Town Hall, Blagrave Street, Reading, Berkshire RG1 1QH

St Albans: The Verulamium Museum, St Michaels, St Albans, Hertfordshire AL3 4SW

York: The Castle Museum, York, YO1 1RY